Chance to Fight

There's still hope
There's still a chance
For you to fight
You can fight for your mistakes
You can fight for your freedom
Fight for your goal!
Learn with your mind
Intelligent comes when you use your eye
In the books
And to study
Listen
God gave you a mouth to speak
But also gave you ears to listen!

Heart Eye

Heart that is with an eye
Show self-made of seeking love
Positive choices
Eye to see the world
Love
Love
Love
Is what my heart says
But being in love with you
Makes my eyes
Stay on you
As a heart eye.

Growing my Heart to be Solid

November 24th
My heart was broken.
Then it started to grow
To be unspoken.
Now my heart has grew
With different actions
That are meaningful

Dark in the Underworld

The rich helps the rich,
And the poor stays the poor.
Standing outside with a sign by the store,
no fight that is given.
No help that is progressing.
Please help the poor!
It will be a true blessing.
Knock
Knock
at the door.
That is sadly locked!
Starving kids begging for food, water,
And hope that is not blocked.
Blocked from our mind that is mental
Which can turn so physical!
Government denies helping the poor
Sadness towards this world.
No help
Guaranteed one strong inspired man
will rise up, and change the world for
the Grape people to accept.

Emotions Break

I have a heart that breaks
Dealing with struggles that cause my emotions to be broken
Anger
Comes
Like a disease
It is contagious
It beats me to my knees
Giving up through life
My emotions is broken
Struggling finding out
What is true in the world?
Heart is broken
There's pieces on the floor
Wondering who is going to
Pick them up?
My emotions remain broken

Lock

The way to find success and love
Is finding the key to adapt to and unlock It
with different meanings

Love and Me

You and me
me and you,
you and love
love and you.
Me and love,
love and me.
Together we love ourselves
which is us
inside are hearts too.

MLK

I had a dream
When you was put laid to rest
All the violence deceased
From all your heart from
Your blood work on the inside.
You gave the fight with
Knowledge,
Power,
Wisdom, and
Standing up for our rights.
Riding through the promised land
God knows when I am going to shake
your hand.
MLK
LALA
I am proud to say
Being black is a perfect way
To let people know my ancestors
From the past

I am thankful that we are free at last.

Our Bodies Tell a Story

Our bodies tells a story
that is filled with so many chapters.
Some won't be pretty,
and some may be.
Take the chance to really read about
how our body tells a story!
Do not tend to judge, we are all not perfect.
Do not tend to budge, wait your turn,
full page, read it.
Some of our chapters are short,
and some pages are long!
Our bodies tell a story
open your "I", and read along.
Read every sentence.
Their mouth is moving with different meanings.
Listen to their story!
Some may not be pretty
our bodies tell a story,
so read then slowly.

Rain That Hits My Lonely Vein

When you take the time to think
The rain hits your lonely vein
Distance yourself from people
More in your brain will gain.
Soon you will gain knowledge, Wisdom,
And speed to chase your dream.
You will remember all the memories,
With people in 2018.
The ones that you left
The ones that died,
Their souls still
Remain a name
Trending worldwide.
Now I am outside
Rain hits my lonely vein
Wondering is it going to be the same
When the sun comes, and
Beam a heat on a mind intelligent
brain.

Soon to Come

Don't chase the recognition,
let the recognition chase you.

Tell Me Who I Am

Define my character!
Is my heart good enough for the world?
My 19 year old self,
that has a mind
that is out of this time.
Writing poetry
do you think doing it for fun is all I am doing?
Define me
Define me
You think being black is what my human mind is *trying* to be?
Negative!
It's what I am!
You define me as a nigga?
Walking in the store you see me
as a violent human figure,
that has the heart to pull out
the gun, and pull the trigger?
Laughing at your answer....
I am just a black male that want to change the world.

The Colorful World

Red goes with blue = fire (and lovely water for you)
White goes with black = black (souls that will come outside at night)
Green goes with blue = (Beautiful grass, and the sky above us meaningful)
Pink goes with white = (Breast cancer we fight, and are souls is holding tight)
Purple goes with gray = (Grapes as we eat, and favorite sharks kids love to see)
Red goes with black = (Broken heart's grow back, but dark)
Yellow goes with yellow = (Gangs that is latin king)
Red goes with red = (Gangs that are blood's)
Blue goes with blue = (Gangs that are crip)
Black goes with white = (The world is blind with full of lies, will there ever be a change?)

The Day I Cry

The day the world change
Will be the day I cry
Because all the poems writing is sparking intelligent
minds,
The day I change the world
Would be the day
shedding tears will come
Because speaking what is real
With passion through my heart to my love ones

The Way The World Hurt Us

The grass is green,
But the world is not as happy as it should be.
The wind is full with so much breeze,
but is this world truthful as it should be?

I don't know man, the system is filled with lies,
have you heard of The Central Park Five?
Their youth were taken away that is filled with sadness.
Locked in a cages for years
for years
for something they did not do,
Which brings tears.
Now they're free!
Being wrongly convicted to the system
Innocent as they always will be.
Disgrace towards Trump
to think they're still guilty!
This world is filled with lies,
And that's how it should not be.

Thoughtful hopes

Guide me to walk
Guide me to write,
Guide me to have hope
Guide me to talk.
Speak when spoken to
without a voice
no one notices you.

Watching a Downfall

Witness my opportunity
that's not taken for granted!
from my former actions which is a true blessing!
Giving up my goal
for another perfect soul, and dame well I hold.
Carrying a lot of responsibilities!
Take a human figure!
Raising a human figure!
Teach the human figure!
Mad intelligent brain will be so bigger,
negative thoughts to the human figure.
Jail time speak upon
d by the gun.
Which he pulls the trigger!
Now in jail!
mind is raising hell,
call for help
crying from your cell

What About My Family ?

All the money in the world
But adapting to wanting my family
All the Christmas love and cheer
But what about my family?
The gifts to be receiving
Spirits is always in me
But I ask again
What about my family ?
Picked up by my mama
Picked up by my daddy
Feelings that are turned cold
Heart will get much better
Family! family! Family!
Found out who's my family
It's all people sitting down
Watching me

What I Thought Was True

Daily living inside my room
Lights above give me grape ideas
Pillow safe for my head
Covers on my bed
Laying thinking ahead
 of time
Sparking intelligent minds
Poems I diagnosed
Hold on one moment
Crumble,
Poverty,
Women,
Black on Black Crime, and
Once upon a time
Now what I thought was true
Equal people would listen
To what is real in society
What's inside of me
Is my reddish heart that beats
That never lies to me
What was true?

What you mean ....what is true?
That people listening to the truth!

When My Time Comes

There may be a chance that when I change the world,
I will not be able to see it.
People do not tend to realize what they have
change until you're gone!
Names will be expressed
while my body laid to rest.

Till now may my chapters go on!
Poems coming along.
Inventions as well!
Let my sins be forgiven,
God forgive me if I fail.

Chance to Fight

There's still hope
There's still a chance
For you to fight
You can fight for your mistakes
You can fight for your freedom
Fight for your goal!
Learn with your mind
Intelligent comes when you use your eye
In the books
And to study
Listen
God gave you a mouth to speak
But also gave you ears to listen!

Heart Eye

Heart that is with an eye
Show self-made of seeking love
Positive choices
Eye to see the world
Love
Love
Love
Is what my heart says
But being in love with you
Makes my eyes
Stay on you
As a heart eye.

Growing my Heart to be Solid

November 24th
My heart was broken.
Then it started to grow
To be unspoken.
Now my heart has grew
With different actions
That are meaningful

Dark in the Underworld

The rich helps the rich,
And the poor stays the poor.
Standing outside with a sign by the store,
no fight that is given.
No help that is progressing.
Please help the poor!
It will be a true blessing.
Knock
Knock
at the door.
That is sadly locked!
Starving kids begging for food, water,
And hope that is not blocked.
Blocked from our mind that is mental
Which can turn so physical!
Government denies helping the poor
Sadness towards this world.
No help
Guaranteed one strong inspired man
will rise up, and change the world for
the Grape people to accept.

Emotions Break

I have a heart that breaks
Dealing with struggles that cause my emotions to be broken
Anger
Comes
Like a disease
It is contagious
It beats me to my knees
Giving up through life
My emotions is broken
Struggling finding out
What is true in the world?
Heart is broken
There's pieces on the floor
Wondering who is going to
Pick them up?
My emotions remain broken

Lock

The way to find success and love
Is finding the key to adapt to and unlock It
with different meanings

Love and Me

You and me
me and you,
you and love
love and you.
Me and love,
love and me.
Together we love ourselves
which is us
inside are hearts too.

MLK

I had a dream
When you was put laid to rest
All the violence deceased
From all your heart from
Your blood work on the inside.
You gave the fight with
Knowledge,
Power,
Wisdom, and
Standing up for our rights.
Riding through the promised land
God knows when I am going to shake
your hand.
MLK
LALA
I am proud to say
Being black is a perfect way
To let people know my ancestors
From the past

I am thankful that we are free at last.

Our Bodies Tell a Story

Our bodies tells a story
that is filled with so many chapters.
Some won't be pretty,
and some may be.
Take the chance to really read about
how our body tells a story!
Do not tend to judge, we are all not perfect.
Do not tend to budge, wait your turn,
full page, read it.
Some of our chapters are short,
and some pages are long!
Our bodies tell a story
open your "I", and read along.
Read every sentence.
Their mouth is moving with different meanings.
Listen to their story!
Some may not be pretty
our bodies tell a story,
so read then slowly.

Rain That Hits My Lonely Vein

When you take the time to think
The rain hits your lonely vein
Distance yourself from people
More in your brain will gain.
Soon you will gain knowledge, Wisdom,
And speed to chase your dream.
You will remember all the memories,
With people in 2018.
The ones that you left
The ones that died,
Their souls still
Remain a name
Trending worldwide.
Now I am outside
Rain hits my lonely vein
Wondering is it going to be the same
When the sun comes, and
Beam a heat on a mind intelligent
brain.

Soon to Come

Don't chase the recognition,
let the recognition chase you.

Tell Me Who I Am

Define my character!
Is my heart good enough for the world?
My 19 year old self,
that has a mind
that is out of this time.
Writing poetry
do you think doing it for fun is all I am doing?
Define me
Define me
You think being black is what my human mind is *trying* to be?
Negative!
It's what I am!
You define me as a nigga?
Walking in the store you see me
as a violent human figure,
that has the heart to pull out
the gun, and pull the trigger?
Laughing at your answer....
I am just a black male that want to change the world.

The Colorful World

Red goes with blue = fire (and lovely water for you)
White goes with black = black (souls that will come outside at night)
Green goes with blue = (Beautiful grass, and the sky above us meaningful)
Pink goes with white = (Breast cancer we fight, and are souls is holding tight)
Purple goes with gray = (Grapes as we eat, and favorite sharks kids love to see)
Red goes with black = (Broken heart's grow back, but dark)
Yellow goes with yellow = (Gangs that is latin king)
Red goes with red = (Gangs that are blood's)
Blue goes with blue = (Gangs that are crip)
Black goes with white = (The world is blind with full of lies, will there ever be a change?)

The Day I Cry

The day the world change
Will be the day I cry
Because all the poems writing is sparking intelligent minds,
The day I change the world
Would be the day
shedding tears will come
Because speaking what is real
With passion through my heart to my love ones

The Way The World Hurt Us

The grass is green,
But the world is not as happy as it should be.
The wind is full with so much breeze,
but is this world truthful as it should be?

I don't know man, the system is filled with lies,
have you heard of The Central Park Five?
Their youth were taken away that is filled with sadness.
Locked in a cages for years
for years
for something they did not do,
Which brings tears.
Now they're free!
Being wrongly convicted to the system
Innocent as they always will be.
Disgrace towards Trump
to think they're still guilty!
This world is filled with lies,
And that's how it should not be.

Thoughtful hopes

Guide me to walk
Guide me to write,
Guide me to have hope
Guide me to talk.
Speak when spoken to
without a voice
no one notices you.

Watching a Downfall

Witness my opportunity
that's not taken for granted!
from my former actions which is a true blessing!
Giving up my goal
for another perfect soul, and dame well I hold.
Carrying a lot of responsibilities!
Take a human figure!
Raising a human figure!
Teach the human figure!
Mad intelligent brain will be so bigger,
negative thoughts to the human figure.
Jail time speak upon
d by the gun.
Which he pulls the trigger!
Now in jail!
mind is raising hell,
call for help
crying from your cell

What About My Family ?

All the money in the world
But adapting to wanting my family
All the Christmas love and cheer
But what about my family?
The gifts to be receiving
Spirits is always in me
But I ask again
What about my family ?
Picked up by my mama
Picked up by my daddy
Feelings that are turned cold
Heart will get much better
Family! family! Family!
Found out who's my family
It's all people sitting down
Watching me

What I Thought Was True

Daily living inside my room
Lights above give me grape ideas
Pillow safe for my head
Covers on my bed
Laying thinking ahead
 of time
Sparking intelligent minds
Poems I diagnosed
Hold on one moment
Crumble,
Poverty,
Women,
Black on Black Crime, and
Once upon a time
Now what I thought was true
Equal people would listen
To what is real in society
What's inside of me
Is my reddish heart that beats
That never lies to me
What was true?

What you mean ....what is true?
That people listening to the truth!

When My Time Comes

There may be a chance that when I change the world,
I will not be able to see it.
People do not tend to realize what they have
change until you're gone!
Names will be expressed
while my body laid to rest.

Till now may my chapters go on!
Poems coming along.
Inventions as well!
Let my sins be forgiven,
God forgive me if I fail.

www.ingramcontent.com/pod-product-compliance
Ingram Content Group UK Ltd.
Pitfield, Milton Keynes, MK11 3LW, UK
UKHW041904190726
13854UKWH00003B/1084

9 780359 806751